Wild Critters
Farm Stories for Wigglers

Jan Crossen

Wild Critters
Farm Stories for Wigglers

Jan Crossen

ISBN: 9798354022342

Copyright 2022, Jan Crossen
All rights reserved. No portion of this book may be reproduced in any form without express written permission from the publisher.
For permission contact: jan@jancrossenauthor.com

Cimarron Pines Publishing
PO Box 696
Lopez Island, WA, USA 98261

Cover and Illustrations by D. Karunarathna

For Darcy, who doesn't have snakes on her Hawaiian island.

It was early evening and Barbara, Linda, and I were relaxing on the back deck enjoying a bowl of homemade ice cream.

"Oh, wow! Look!" I whispered, pointing towards the edge of the pasture where it meets the forest. "There's a mommy deer, and she has two babies!"

Have you ever seen a baby deer? Did you know that a baby deer is called a fawn?

-05-

"Welcome, little ones," Barbara said.

Suddenly, something scared the deer and all three ran away and quickly disappeared into the woods. We went back to eating our ice cream.

Do you like ice cream? What's your favorite flavor?

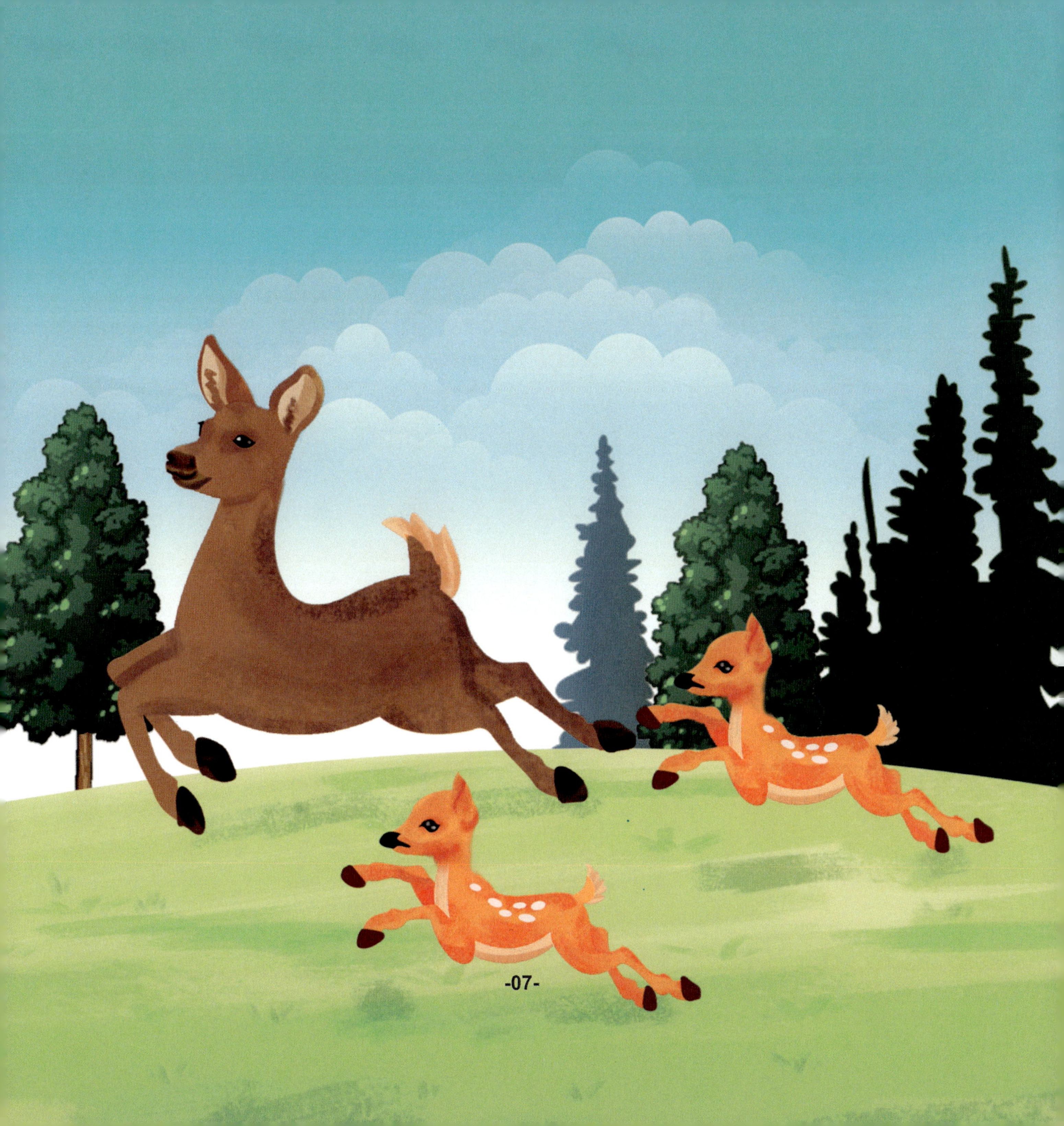

Barbara, Linda, and I live on a small farm on an island. An island is land that has water all around it. There are a lot of other islands near where we live. Have you ever been to an island?

-09-

Orca whales live near our island. These whales are big black and white animals that live in the water. They swim, eat, sleep, and play with their parents, brothers, sisters, cousins, aunts, uncles, and grandparents. Orcas talk with each other by making clicking sounds and whistling calls. Do you know how to whistle?

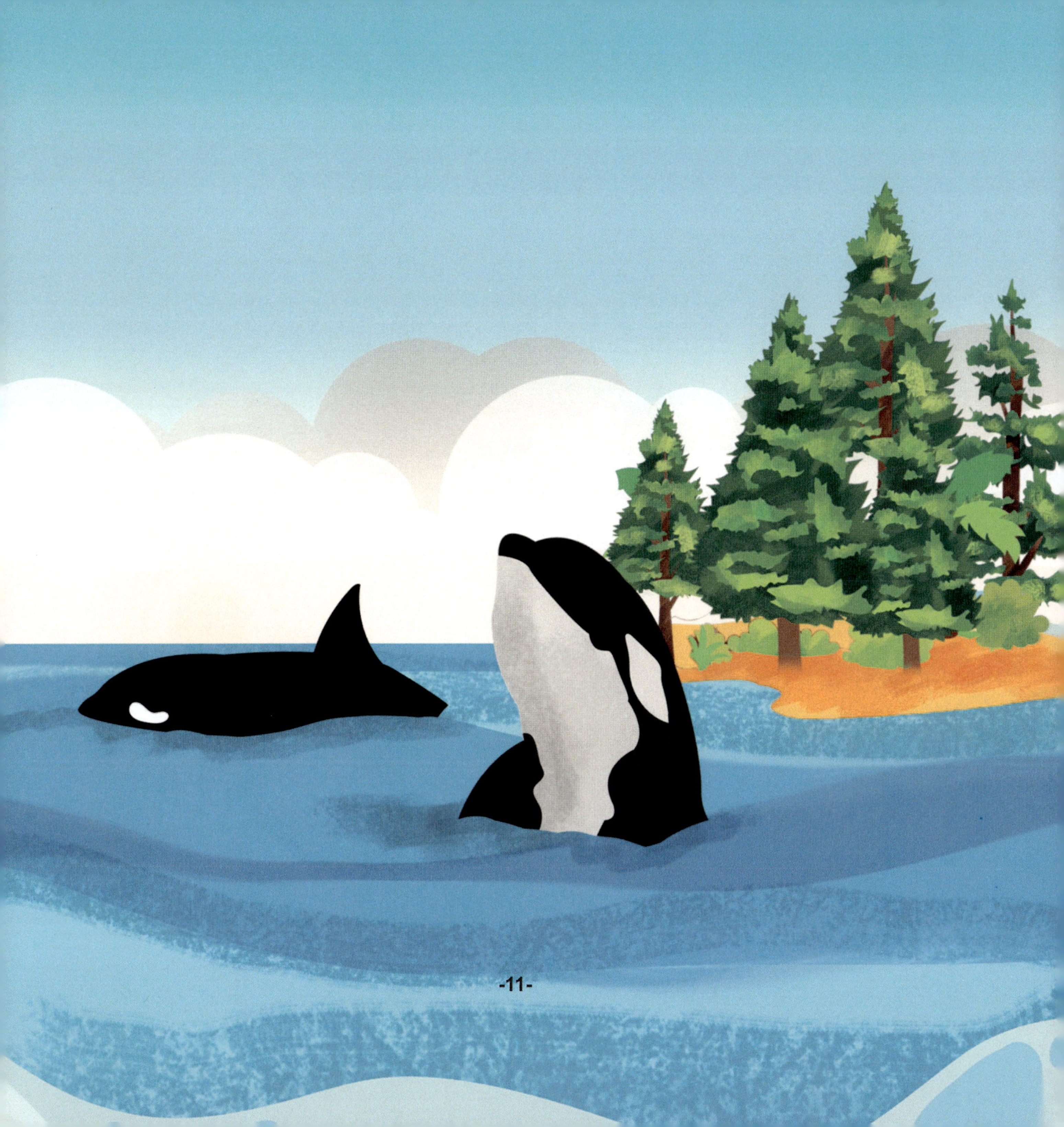

Because Barbara, Linda, and I live in the country and not a city, we see a lot of different kinds of wild animals near our house. We really like watching the Black-tailed deer.

These deer have brown hair, tall ears, and tails that are black and white. Black-tailed deer are great swimmers. They can even swim between the islands! Have you learned how to swim yet?

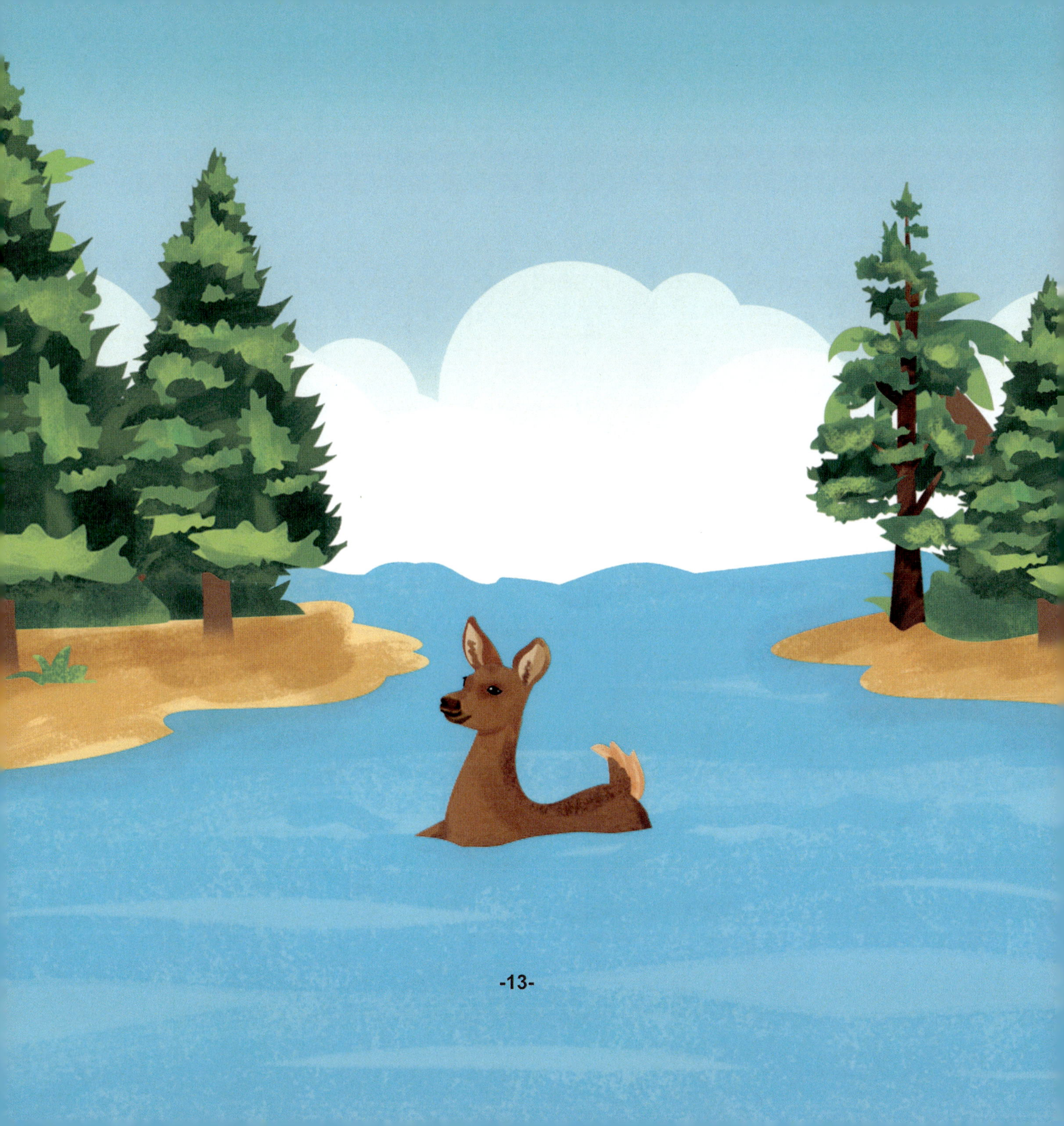

"Look over there," I said, "that looks like 'Tears' standing just inside the forest." I pointed towards a grown-up deer.

"I see him," said Barbara. "He has big antlers on his head!"

We named him, "Tears," because he has white markings under his eyes that look like tear drops. Don't worry, though, he hasn't been crying. He's a happy deer!

-15-

"Now look over that way," I said, pointing in another direction. "I think that's 'Batman' heading our way."

"Batman" is a younger deer who has a dark marking on his forehead that reminds us of the famous Batman signal. Do you know who Batman is?

-17-

"Barbara, would you please tell me again about deer and their antlers?" Linda asked.

"Sure," said Barbara. "Antlers are those stick-like things on top of the head of the boy deer. Antlers are made of bone. The deer wear antlers for most of the year but after a while, they drop their antlers and leave them on the ground. That's okay because in a couple of months, they start growing new antlers all over again."

-19-

"I like finding antlers that the deer have dropped," I said. "I've found them in our pastures and in the woods."

"Antlers come is different shapes and sizes," Linda said. "Some are straight and pointed, and others look like tree branches."

"Hang on," I said. "I'm going to go get the antlers that we've found. I'll be right back."

I went inside and grabbed our small collection of antlers and brought them outside. We looked at them while we finished our dessert.

Have you ever seen a real deer antler?

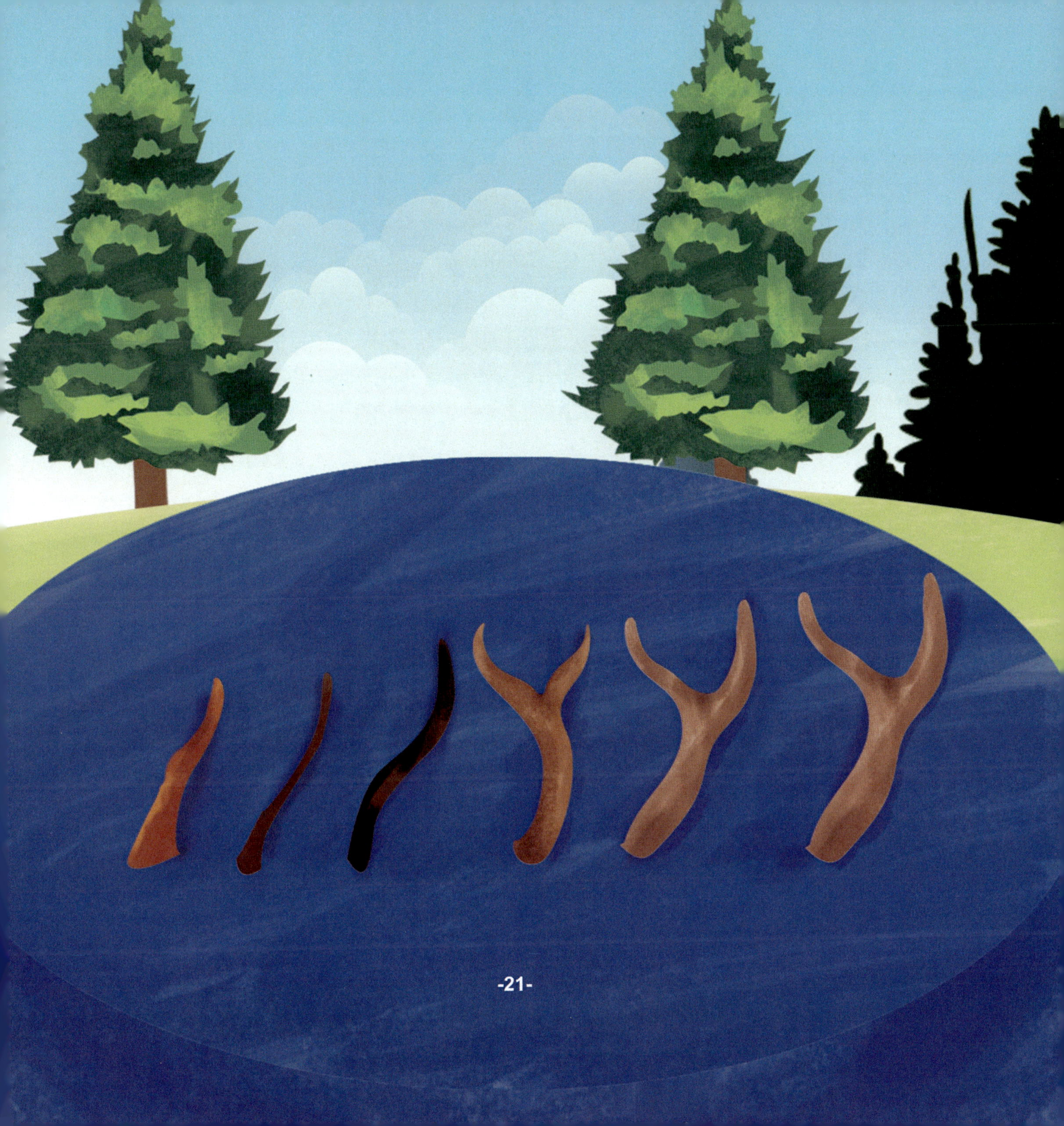

Early the next morning Barbara and I went outside to do our farm chores. Doing our farm chores means that we are taking care of our animals. We are feeding them, making sure they have clean water and fresh bedding, and cleaning up after them.

Sometimes we sing songs to them while we work. We made up special songs to sing to them. Do you have pets? Do you ever make up songs and sing to them?

-23-

While doing our chores, we spotted a gray squirrel climbing down the garden fence. He has a thick, bushy tail, and his coat is a mixture of gray, brown, white, and black fur.

"Look," I said. "He's carrying a red apple in his mouth!"

"I see that," said Barbara. "And he's running across the pasture towards the forest."

We watched as the squirrel scurried out of sight with his apple.

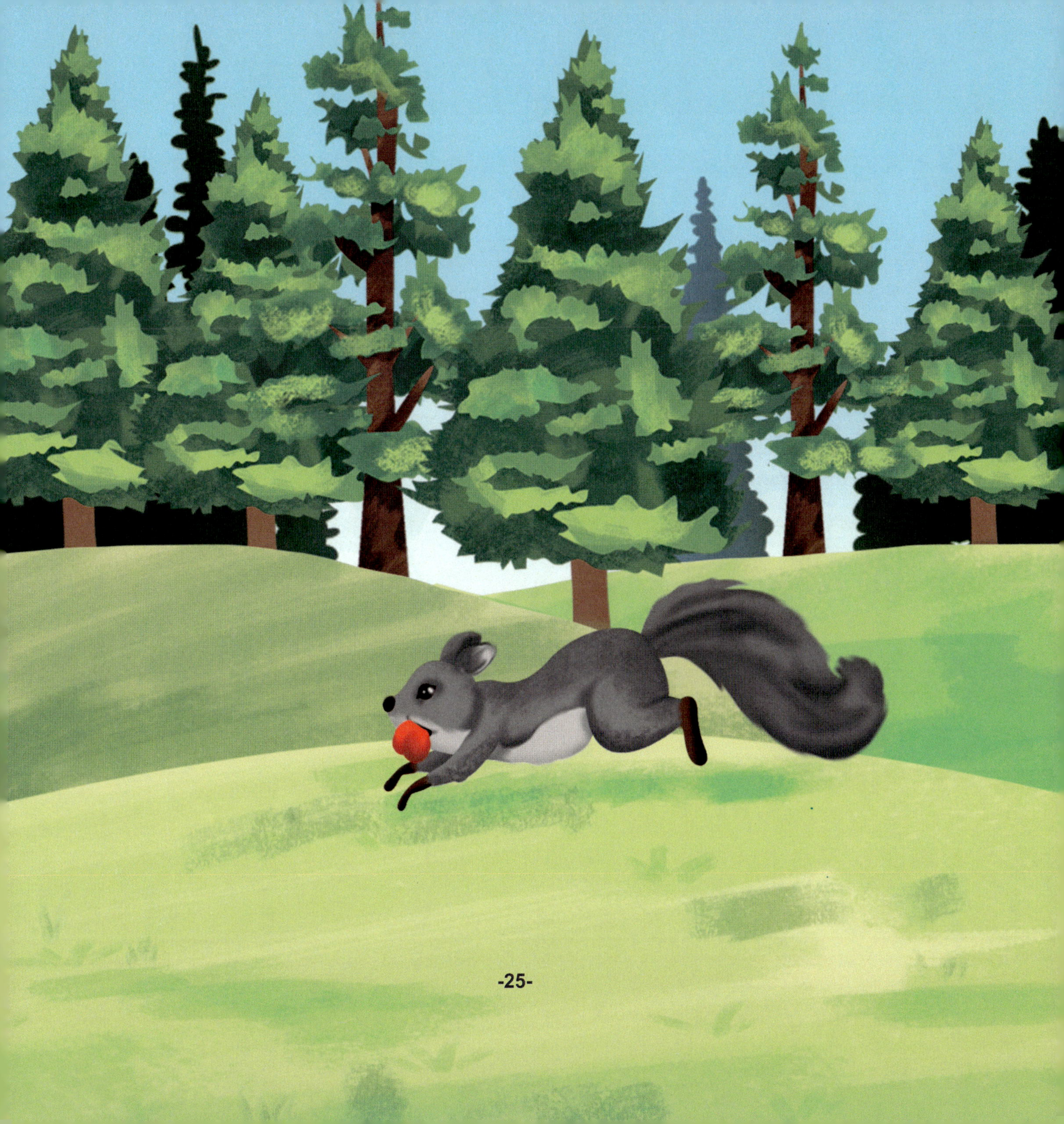

"If he's getting apples from the garden, I bet he's also eating seeds from the birdfeeder," I said.

"Let's get him some unsalted, unroasted peanuts," Barbara said. "We can leave them under the tree for him."

"Great idea," I agreed. "It will be fun to watch him find and eat the peanuts."

-27-

Barbara and I split up and I went to take care of the horses while she went off to care for the cows. I was at the horse's water trough when I spotted something that made me catch my breath and jump back. It was a striped garter snake. Luckily, all the snakes on our island are non-poisonous. Garter snakes are good for gardens but don't touch! They can sometimes bite. It's best to just leave them alone.

-29-

Early the next morning I found Barbara standing on the back deck.

"Look," she said, and pointed towards a Barred Owl sitting on the branch of a nearby tree.

A Barred Owl is a large bird with a gentle looking face, big wings, and very sharp claws. We got a good, long look at the owl, and he studied us too. After a few minutes the owl spread his wings and flew away. Barbara and I waved goodbye.

-31-

"Because we live in the country we see a lot of different wildlife," Barbara said.

"Yes," I said. "I love seeing wild critters like the deer and squirrels, and amazing birds like that Barred Owl."

"Don't forget the snakes," Barbara added, moving her arm as if it were a snake slithering across the ground.

"Yes," I said. "I'm even grateful for snakes. Every critter has its place in the world. I want each one to live a happy life and be exactly who he is meant to be."

-33-

THE END

If you enjoyed **Wild Critters on the Farm**, it would mean so much if you would take a minute to leave your kind words as a review on Amazon. Parents, grandparents, teachers, and librarians rely on honest feedback from others when they make their buying decisions.

"Jan's stories invite a child to snuggle in and listen to these wonderful stories. I highly recommend all her books.
"Patricia L. Sands, Award-winning Women's Fiction Writer

Acknowledgment:
Thanks, always, to my Honey B for her continued love and support. I couldn't do this without you, nor would I want to try.

Meet Jan Crossen:
Jan is a **gold level Mom's Choice Award-winning author** who writes books about special people and animals that have touched her heart and life. She invites you to visit her website at www.jancrossenauthor.com.

Please follow her on her author page on Amazon, Facebook, BookBub, and Instagram at Jan Crossen, Author. Jan would love to hear from you and can be reached at jan@jancrossenauthor.com

Additional read aloud picture books for ages 3-5:

America's Heartland, the TV show
Says kids today just do not know
About crops and animals; life on the farm
Let them experience some country charm.

Farm Stories for Wigglers is a fun and entertaining read aloud series. Your little ones will delight in these interactive stories and there are even a couple with fun songs! Gather your kids and grab a book; come visit our little farm! The books in this "Wiggler's" series include:
- **Wilbur the Cat**
- **Julip the Cow**
- **Orchid the Horse**
- **Pearl, the Wonder Horse**
- **Little Chickens**
- **Four Laughing Duckies**
- **Wild Critters on the Farm**

Blind and abandoned for 30 days
Hungry, scared; she was all alone.
Then kind strangers came to her rescue
Now she has a forever home.

A Forever Home for Glori
This is a tender, read aloud picture book that is sure to become a favorite of youngsters. This beautifully illustrated book is a true story about love and second chances.

FOREVER
He was a foster child needing a family and she was a woman wanting a child. This is the true story of the night they met. Their journey began as they enjoyed the magnificent displays of holiday lights together, and ended with him jumping from foster care into the arms of this woman who would love and keep him forever.

Jan Crossen has entertaining and informative books for early readers **ages 6-9** as well. They include:

Glori, Miracle Dog

The Farm Adventures Series:

- **-The Adventures of Wilbur, A Part-time Farm Cat**
- **- My Musical Cow**
- **- Dream Horse**
- **- White Lightning**
- **- Chick-a-dee-doo-dah**
- **- Superpowered Ducks**
- **- Deer Haven Farm**

Made in the USA
Middletown, DE
28 October 2022